# Piano Love Songs FOR DUMMIES

**Performance Notes by Bob Gulla
and Willie Myette**

ISBN: 978-1-4234-4040-6

Visit Hal Leonard Online at
**www.halleonard.com**

# Table of Contents

· · · · · · · · · · · · · · · · · · · · · · · · · · · · · · · · · · · · ·

# Introduction

Hopeless romantics, welcome to *Piano Love Songs For Dummies!* In this enduring collection we show you how to play some of popular music's very finest love songs. What a beautiful thing! We're pretty sure you'll find many of your favorites, but we're also guessing you'll discover music you may not have considered learning on piano. Perhaps (gasp!) you will even fall in love with a song!

If you're a sucker for a great love song, like we are, it won't be too hard to find oodles to like here. There are so many classics to dig into, from the opening "Always" by Irving Berlin right through Elton John's "Your Song." Along the way, you can tackle great tunes like Lionel Richie's "Lady," (and find out what happened after he gave that tune to Kenny Rogers); "What the World Needs Now Is Love," the Bacharach tune popularized by Jackie DeShannon; John Lennon's "Woman" and Lennon and McCartney's "Here, There and Everywhere." The list is long and luxurious, and the book clicks like a great relationship.

The songs in this collection are suitable for a wide range of abilities, from beginners to more experienced players. As you explore these pages and paddle down this virtual "Tunnel of Love," we're sure you'll gain a new appreciation for what makes a great love song. Conversely, if you, the hopeless romantic, ask yourself, "Hmmm, I wonder what exactly makes a great love song?" you'll find the answers right here, more than three dozen of them!

## About This Book

For every song here, we include a little background or history. We discuss the artist, the song, or some other interesting element. This information is followed by a variety of tidbits that struck us as we made our way through the teaching of these songs, including some of the following:

✔ A run-down of the parts you need to know.

✔ A breakdown of some of the chord progressions important to playing the song effectively.

✔ Some of the critical information you need to navigate the music.

✔ Some tips and shortcuts you can use to expedite the learning process.

In many cases, you may already know how to do a lot of this. If so, feel free to skip over those familiar bits.

## How to Use This Book

The music in this book is in standard piano notation — a staff for the melody and lyrics above the traditional piano grand staff. We assume you know a little something about reading music, and that you know a little bit about playing piano — such as how to hold your fingers, basic chords, and how to look cool while doing it. If you need a refresher course on piano, please check out *Piano For Dummies* by Blake Neely (Wiley).

We recommend that you first play through the song, and then practice all the main sections and chords. From there, you can add the tricks and treats of each one — and there are many. Approach each song one section at a time and then assemble them together in a sequence. This technique helps to provide you with a greater understanding of how the song is structured, and enables you to play it through more quickly.

In order to follow the music and our performance notes, you need a basic understanding of scales and chords. But if you're not a wiz, don't worry. Just spend a little time with the nifty tome *Music Theory For Dummies* by Michael Pilhofer and Holly Day (Wiley), and with a little practice, you'll be on your way to entertaining family and friends.

# Glossary

As you might expect, we use quite a few musical terms in this book. Some of these may be unfamiliar to you, so here are a few right off the bat that can help your understanding of basic playing principles:

- **Accidental:** Sharps, flats, or naturals that alter pitches in the key signature.

- **Arpeggio:** Playing the notes of a chord one at a time rather than all together.

- **Bridge:** Part of the song that is different from the verse and the chorus, providing variety and connecting the other parts of the song to each other.

- **Coda:** The section at the end of a song, which is sometimes labeled with the word "coda."

- **Hook:** A familiar, accessible, or sing-along melody, lick, or other section of the song.

- **Progression:** A series of chords played in succession.

- **Slash chord:** A chord with a specific bass note listed to the right of the chord name: C/G, for example.

- **Walking bass line:** Steady, step-wise movement played by the upright bass or piano if there is no other bass instrument.

# Icons Used in This Book

In the margins of this book are lots of little icons that will help make your life easier:

A reason to stop and review advice that can prevent personal injury to your fingers, your brain, or your ego.

These are optional parts, or alternate approaches that those who'd like to find their way through the song with a distinctive flair can take. Often these are slightly more challenging routes, but encouraged nonetheless, because there's nothing like a good challenge!

This is where you will find notes about specific musical concepts that are relevant but confusing to non-musical types — stuff that you wouldn't bring up, say, at a frat party or at your kid's soccer game.

You get lots of these tips, because the more playing suggestions we can offer, the better you'll play. And isn't that what it's all about?

# Always

Words and Music by Irving Berlin

**Moderate Waltz**

Ev - 'ry - thing went wrong, and the whole day long ___ I'd
Dreams will all come true, grow - ing old with you, ___ and

feel so blue. ___
time will fly, ___

# Always on My Mind

Words and Music by Wayne Thompson, Mark James and Johnny Christopher

# Baby, I Love Your Way

Words and Music by Peter Frampton

# And I Love Her

Words and Music by John Lennon and Paul McCartney

End instrumental solo

And I love

her.

# And I Love You So

Words and Music by Don McLean

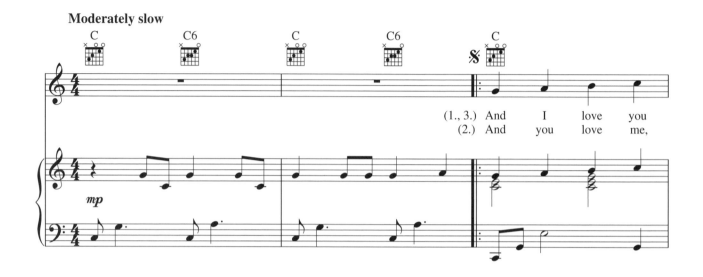

know.
do.

I guess they un‑der‑stand
The book of life is brief,

how lone‑ly life has been,
and once a page is read,

but life be‑gan a‑
all but love is

gain,
dead,

the day you took my hand.
that is my be‑lief.

# Beautiful in My Eyes

Words and Music by Joshua Kadison

# Best of My Love

Words and Music by John David Souther, Don Henley and Glenn Frey

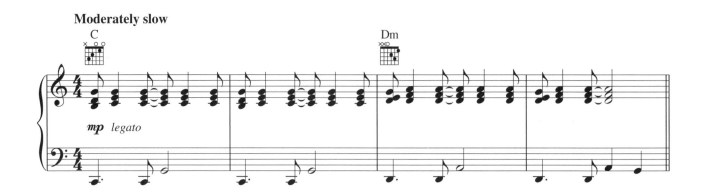

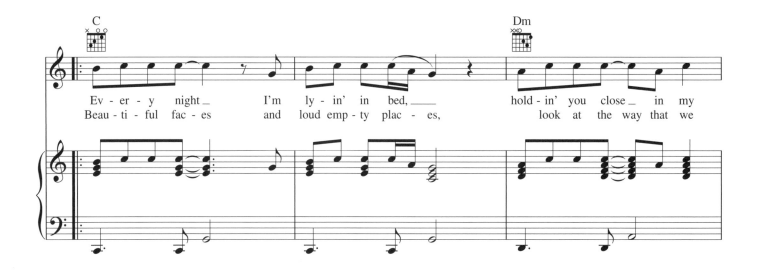

# Can't Help Falling in Love

Words and Music by George David Weiss, Hugo Peretti and Luigi Creatore

# Can You Feel the Love Tonight

from Walt Disney Pictures' THE LION KING
Music by Elton John
Lyrics by Tim Rice

# Can't Smile Without You

Words and Music by Chris Arnold, David Martin and Geoff Morrow

# (They Long to Be) Close to You

Lyric by Hal David
Music by Burt Bacharach

# A Groovy Kind of Love

Words and Music by Toni Wine and Carole Bayer Sager

# Here, There and Everywhere

Words and Music by John Lennon and Paul McCartney

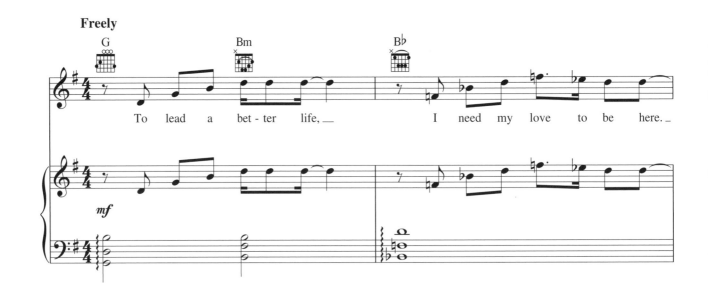

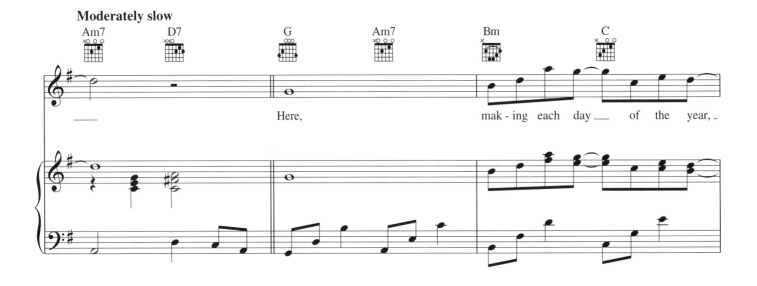

# How Deep Is the Ocean (How High Is the Sky)

Words and Music by Irving Berlin

# I Left My Heart in San Francisco

Words by Douglass Cross
Music by George Cory

# I Will

### Words and Music by John Lennon and Paul McCartney

# I'll Be There

Words and Music by Berry Gordy, Hal Davis, Willie Hutch and Bob West

# I'll Have to Say I Love You in a Song

Words and Music by Jim Croce

# Isn't It Romantic?

from the Paramount Picture LOVE ME TONIGHT
Words by Lorenz Hart
Music by Richard Rodgers

# If

Words and Music by David Gates

**Moderately, with feeling**

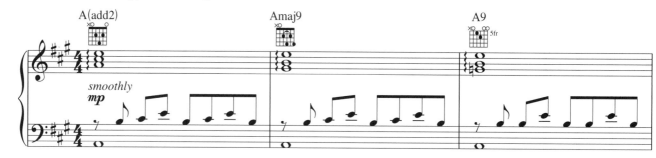

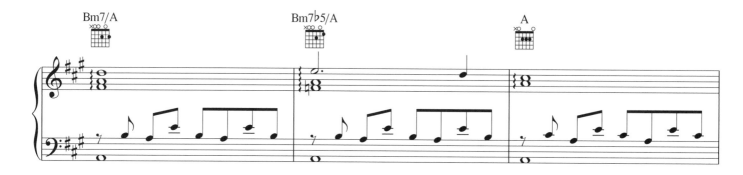

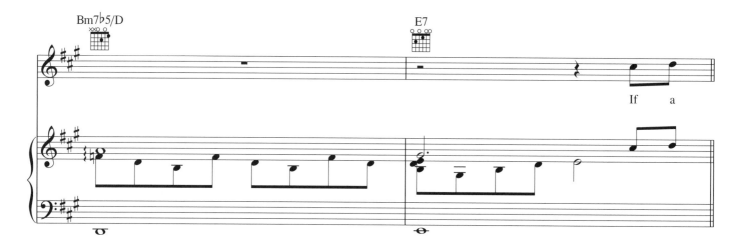

If a
pic  -  ture paints a thou  -  sand words, __ then why __
man could be two plac  -  es at __ one time, __

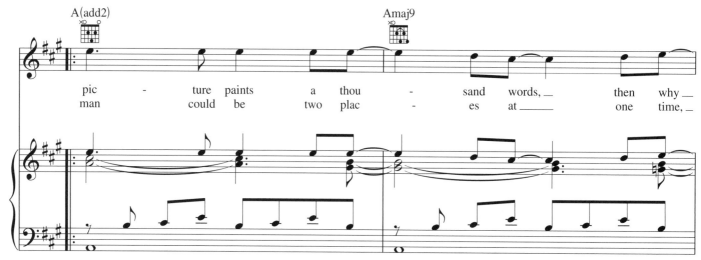

## If I Loved You

from CAROUSEL

Lyrics by Oscar Hammerstein II
Music by Richard Rodgers

# Performance Notes

## *Always* (page 6)

Irving Berlin was a master at saying "I Love You" in 32 bars. He was so good at it that Cole Porter dubbed an entire genre of 20th century love songs the "Berlin ballad." Berlin wrote "Always" in 1925 for Ellin Mackay, the woman he married that same year. Berlin already had success as a songwriter, including "Alexander's Ragtime Band," which some call the first real American musical work. Anyway, Berlin wrote "Always" for Mackay and pledged the song's royalties to her, which would become considerable. Out of the gate, two artists hit the top spot with it on separate occasions, and then there were four more hits in the '40s. In the '60s, it became country singer Patsy Cline's posthumous anthem. Not that MacKay needed the cash. She was already a Park Avenue heiress.

Keep it loose when playing this beautiful waltz. Don't be afraid to add a little "lilt" to the rhythm. Try singing the lyrics to yourself a few times and make sure that you don't sound robotic. Ella Fitzgerald sang a beautiful rendition of this song in the '50s. Try mimicking her singing in your playing.

It's easy to rush a waltz. Don't! A good rule of thumb: No matter how slow you're playing, you're probably still playing too fast! Try experimenting by playing this song *extremely* slow. In fact, try taking a short breath between bars to add just a little bit more space. Classical pianists do this all the time, they have fun with the tempo; and you can too!

Even though it is not written, you can *roll* some of your chords for effect. You do this by starting on the bottom note and quickly rolling up to the top note. You don't want to do this for all of your chords. Instead, choose points of interest within the song in which to roll your chords. For example, try rolling your chords each time the lyric is "Always . . ."

## *Always on My Mind* (page 10)

First recorded by Brenda Lee, this little song has had quite a journey. A collaboration between songwriters Mark James, Wayne Carson, and Johnny Christopher, the tune took a few years to attract attention. Lee never had a hit with it, but Elvis did, recorded as a B side to his single "Separate Ways." Oddly enough, "Always" was issued as the A side in the UK, where it became a hit, and "Separate Ways" served as the B side. Anyway, from there the song gained momentum, mainly in the country vein. Warbler Willie Nelson racked up all kinds of awards with his 1982 version, chosen as the #1 country song of 1982. Over 300 artists have recorded it.

*Ledger lines* are used to write musical notes outside of the typical five lines and four spaces of the staff. It can be challenging to read all those ledger lines. Here's a tip: Look at the chord symbol written above the lyrics. Right at the beginning, in bar 2, you see a note in the left hand written four ledger lines below the staff. It might take you a while to see that this note is F. Guess what? The chord written above the lyrics is an F chord. So, next time you see all those ledger lines look at the chord symbol. It's probably the note you're looking for!

Don't be fooled by the term *slow ballad.* There is a beat here, so don't be shy! It's okay to think of this as a rock ballad. To be effective when playing a ballad like this, you don't want to bang away at the piano. Keep that steady 4/4 pulse in your head and pretend to hear the snare hitting on the backbeat (beats 2 and 4). This will help you accent the chords and propel the song.

The right-hand notes in the beginning on "treat you" are quite a stretch. The notes are G, C, and A. This creates an interval of a 9th. Depending on the size of your hand, this might be quite a stretch to play all those notes at once. That squiggly line in front of the notes tells you to *arpeggiate,* or break up the notes of the chord. So, instead of playing them all at once, you start with the bottom note G and move up to A, playing each note individually.

# And I Love Her (page 18)

Paul McCartney wrote the majority of this song with a little help from John Lennon. Paul took his romantic inspiration from Jane Asher, his love interest at the time (he actually wrote the song in her basement). Lennon and McCartney wrote quite a few songs during their middle period in the Asher basement. Lennon called this song "Paul's first 'Yesterday,'" in that it was a big ballad, and the central romantic moment on the band's album *A Hard Day's Night*. The Beatles began recording the song on February 25, 1964. They recorded two takes that day, with a full electric line-up, then changed course and quieted it down. Although it became one of The Beatles' most admired recordings following its release, the group only performed it once live; outside Abbey Road, for a UK radio show.

The Beatles were masters at doing a lot with a little. After the introduction, the first six bars of this song are only two chords. The left hand is playing a classic rock bass rhythm but the right-hand melody is syncopated ever so nicely against that bass line. Rhythm is the foundation of this song. Start by playing the left-hand rhythm for the bars "I give her all my love" using only the note F in the left hand. Do the same for the rhythm of the lyrics; use your right hand and only the note F. Next try putting them together. Challenging? Practice this a few times to get down the syncopated rhythm of this song.

The E6 chord in the first and second endings, along with the F6 chord on the last page in the first ending can sound harsh if played all at the same volume or intensity level. When you see repeated chords (or notes) try varying the dynamics of those chords. For instance, the rhythm includes two quarter notes and four eighth notes. To add variety, try getting softer as you play the four eighth notes. Alternatively, you can break up the notes of the chord and arpeggiate the chord. So, instead of playing B, C♯, E, and G♯ together four times in a row, break them up!

Save up your volume for the coda! At the coda, we move up a half step to the key of F major. When we move to a new key, we are modulating. Often, a *modulation* (especially when moving up) is matched with a change in dynamics. Next time you hear a singer *modulate* or *change keys*, listen for that "little something extra" in the volume. To achieve this yourself, start the song a little softer than you normally would so that you can get a little louder at the coda.

# And I Love You So (page 22)

Songwriter Don McLean is known for a few enduring songs, including, of course, "American Pie" and "Vincent," his tribute to Vincent Van Gogh. McLean recorded "And I Love You So" for his debut album, *Tapestry,* back in 1970, and released this song as a single. Unfortunately, this one didn't go anywhere of note, let alone make it to the charts. Soon, though, others began latching onto McLean's material. Crooner Perry Como took this tune to the top of the charts in 1973 (it was Como's last Top 40 single), and Elvis recorded it in 1975. Elvis loved the song so much he performed it live until his death two years later.

The left hand arpeggios are by far the most challenging aspect of this arrangement. If you have difficulty with them, break them down! Try playing the first two notes. Next, add another note. Keep looping that pattern. For instance, before the first ending, the notes are D, A, F, A, C, A, F, A. Quite a few notes huh? Try playing only the D, A, F for a few minutes, and then add one note at a time to achieve a sweet legato sound!

Use pedal, but don't put the pedal to the metal! The flowing arpeggios deserve some sustain pedal to create a smooth (*legato*, which means "tied together" in Italian) effect. But don't go overboard! Try putting the pedal down at the beginning of bar 4, but lift the pedal before it starts to sound too "ringy."

# Baby, I Love Your Way *(page 13)*

Peter Frampton, with his blonde leonine tresses, paid ten years worth of dues before earning payback by becoming one of the '70s biggest arena rock stars. Before he ruled the charts with his epic double live album *Frampton Comes Alive!*, this British guitar hero bounced around from band to band. He grabbed session work when he could and set out as a solo artist. His third solo album, *Frampton*, came out in 1975 and was the first of Frampton's work to really grab anyone's attention. But it wasn't until *Alive* that songs from that album like "Show Me the Way" and "Baby, I Love Your Way" began their takeover of radio stations everywhere.

Ah, a rock tune in the key of G. This key fits so well on the piano, but a bunch of 16th and 32nd notes in this tune may trip you up! Hearing a rock drum beat in your head will help you keep the beat. Try warming up by playing 16th notes on G in the right hand while walking down the G major scale in the left hand. You're listening for a strong, steady pulse that sounds rocking, so keep that drum beat going in your head.

Do yourself a favor and take a look at the solo in the second ending. Don't let those 32nd notes scare you. The passage under the D/F♯ chord is filled with 32nd-note goodness, so take a look now to keep from being surprised later!

Watch out for that runaway train! Rock tunes are easy to speed up but ever so difficult to slow down, so keep that steady beat without rushing.

# Beautiful in My Eyes *(page 26)*

Joshua Kadison left home at 16, shortly after his mother died, with the aim of becoming something of a traveling troubadour. He played whenever and wherever, and for whomever he could. It was a period of intense discovery, a time in which Joshua learned a lot about himself; and his experiences suffused his songs. During this musical enrichment, one of the most significant things he did was apprentice with Otelia Monterrey, a Native American medicine woman. She began teaching Joshua the healing principles of sound. He found he was soon spending more time studying than recording and he became Otelia's full-time student. "I thought I knew something about sound," he said in an interview at the time. "Now I know that I know nothing, and I'm excited by the possibilities." His soul traveled the path with Otelia for three years, until her death. "It was the strangest thing really," he said. "She found me as much as I found her. She told me I would be her last student, and I didn't know what she meant until she died."

Don't rush this popular song. You should have the steady backbeat in your head while playing so that you get the accents just right. To get the feel, play the right-hand part while tapping beats 2 and 4 with your left hand on your lap. Watch out for changing time signatures in the coda. There is a bar of 2/4 time just before the end of the song.

Get your rock 'n' roll lighter ready. Did you know that you can double notes to get a bigger sound? The intro is a perfect spot for this. Try playing the left-hand F, G, A♭, and B♭ in octaves. To avoid a crash with the right hand, double an octave below the notes written.

# Best of My Love (page 30)

Glenn Frey and J.D. Souther, two of this song's co-writers, met in Los Angeles in the late '60s, moved into an apartment above soon-to-be friend Jackson Browne, and formed a band called the Longbranch Pennywhistle. Obviously, with a name like that, nothing really came of the act, and they both began seeking out other creative outlets. Souther teamed up with Chris Hillman and Richie Furay to form the more credible country rock band Souther Hillman Furay Band. And Frey, of course, joined Don Henley (the third co-writer) as a member of the Eagles. But Frey and Souther kept in touch over the years and enjoyed much fruitful and lucrative collaboration, including well-known tracks like "Best of My Love," "Heartache Tonight," and "New Kid in Town," all of which helped to define the Eagles' legendary folk/rock hybrid — and country rock in general.

Relax into this song because this is a slow rock song that is easy to play too fast. Start by playing only the bass line (left hand). The dotted rhythm in the bass might be a little tricky at first, so be patient.

If you look at the left-hand pattern in the introduction, you have C, C, and G held for two beats. To help fill out the bar, try playing another G on beat 4 an octave lower. So, the new bass line would be C, C, G, G.

# Can You Feel the Love Tonight (page 38)

"Hakuna Matata" indeed. That's what Elton was singing, figuratively anyway, after *The Lion King*, his collaboration with songwriter Tim Rice, hit the jackpot in 1995. Of the five nominees for Best Song at that year's Academy Awards®, three of them were from this soundtrack. You recall the third tune, right? That would be "Circle of Life." "Can You Feel the Love Tonight" won Best Song, but we're pretty sure everyone involved with that film and its soundtrack felt like winners. It remained atop the *Billboard* charts for nine weeks and went on to sell 15 million units!

The inner chords written in the treble clef might be a "tongue-twister" for your hands. You might be tempted to play the B♭ and E♭ with the stems down in bar 5 with your right hand, but did you know you could also use your left hand instead? Remember, you have two hands, so even though the notes are written in the treble clef, the left can still lend a helping, well, hand.

Want to try your hand at re-arranging the song? Yes, you can do it! At the very end of the song, at "believe the ver-y best," go back to the introduction and play the first 3 bars up to the B♭/D chord, then play the last bar of the song. By "copying and pasting" you can come up with your own arrangement. Cool!

# Can't Help Falling in Love (page 35)

Luigi Creatore and Hugo Peretti shared a small office in New York City's original songwriting factory, the Brill Building. They were under contract to RCA, which meant they had access to artists like Sam Cooke, The Isley Brothers, and Perry Como, for whom they produced five consecutive albums. But they really hit the big time when another RCA artist, Elvis Presley, chose to cover a Hugo and Luigi tune, this one written with George Weiss, called "Can't Help Falling in Love." The song would become a signature piece for Presley, originally appearing in the film *Blue Hawaii* and the album of the same name.

During Presley's late '60s and early '70s performances, the song invariably served as the show's finale. It was also performed in the live segment of his famous 1968 NBC television special, and as the closer for his 1973 Global telecast, "Aloha from Hawaii." Incidentally, Perry Como did a nice rendition of the song himself, but nothing, no matter how genius, would measure up to the King's own version.

On the second page, the Am to E7 chord under "Like a river flows" might be tricky at first, especially the E7 chord on beat 2. Yes, that is an F♮ on the E7 chord, which makes an E7♭9 chord. If that chord sounds too weird to your ears, just change that F to an E and you've got a perfectly fine E7 chord.

Think of the blue seas of Hawaii when playing this arrangement. The inner notes (stems down in the right-hand starting on line 2) should be played gently. Even if a note gets "lost at sea" because you played too softly, that's okay. It's all about the flow!

# Can't Smile Without You (page 42)

Does it strike you as odd that this song appeared at a key moment in the film *Hellboy II?* But there it is, in all its ascending keys glory, playing, somewhat ironically in a scene between Hellboy and Abe Sapien. The scene itself resonates with emotional honesty — the viewer gets to eavesdrop on a very human moment between a demon with his horns shaved off, and, well, a humanoid fish. Although the scene itself rings true with emotion, it is seriously, humorously undercut by Manilow's boisterous love song. We're not sure how the producers of the film sold Manilow, generally an earnest artist, on using one of his better-known tracks in such an unorthodox sense. But there it is in *Hellboy II* with weird monster-type characters. But don't let that ghoulish vision influence the way you hear this song. If you can help it, that is.

Holy key changes Batman! There are, count 'em, three key changes in this song! We start in the key of G, and then go up in half steps till we settle at Bb. The first key change starts on the third page of this arrangement. Practice the bar before each key change for a smooth transition.

Much of this song has an "oom-pah" feel to it. Starting on the Gmaj7 chord in bar 5, you'll notice that the left hand moves between the root G and the fifth D. This is a common accompaniment technique and is really fun to play! Make sure that you don't play the *inner chord*, which is the one with the down stems in the right hand, too loudly. That inner chord should just have a nice "bounce" to it and be a bit softer.

# (They Long to Be) Close to You (page 48)

Burt Bacharach and Hal David penned this gem way back in the early '60s, some seven years before Karen and Richard Carpenter got their meat hooks into it and took it to the top of the charts. As the story goes, Richard Carpenter, the one with the big smile on the keyboards and the de facto decision-maker of the band, didn't really dig the idea of covering the song. But his label chief, A&M's Herb Alpert did a little arm-twisting, and the song eventually became a #1 single in 1970 and a GRAMMY® winner for Best Contemporary Performance. The Carpenters would go on to win two more GRAMMYs, and they followed up this hit with the equally smashing "We've Only Just Begun." Talk about a one-two punch! Actually, it's more like a one-two "love tap," but still.

Don't be stiff! Be sure to swing those eighth notes. To swing the eighth notes you can think of them as triplets with the middle note omitted. *Triplets* are three "attacks" in one beat and sound like this: trip-a-let, trip-a-let, and so on. If you omit the middle triplet, you get: trip-let. You can also think "long-short, long-short" to get the groove.

Watch for the key change on the third page! You're moving from the key of G up a half step to the key of A♭. If you want to add more motion to the bass line you can play the same root-fifth bass pattern from the previous page.

# A Groovy Kind of Love (page 54)

When it comes to songwriting, sometimes the path of least resistance is best, and so it was with Carole Bayer Sager and Toni Wine's mid-1960s ditty "Groovy Kind of Love." Composed at the piano with Wine and Sager banging it out, riffing on simple chords and lyrical phrases, the song was written in 20 minutes. From there it took on a life of its own, spawning scores of renditions from artists like Petula Clark, the Mindbenders, Sonny & Cher, and Phil Collins. In fact, the list incorporates pretty much everyone you can envision singing the word "groovy" in a song. Collins recorded his version in 1988, well past the time that particular word was still in use. It didn't matter. The former drummer had a hit with it anyway.

Watch out for the key change on the second page. You're moving from the key of G to the key of A. This is cool because many rock songs move up by half-steps; this one moves up by a whole step. Also, be aware of the difference in rhythms in the second ending leading to the key change. Do you see how the right-hand G chord has a dotted quarter–two eighths–dotted quarter rhythm? In the following bar the right-hand D chord has a slightly different rhythm, so watch out!

If you want to add more movement to the left-hand bass line, try playing the bass line in quarter notes rather than holding out the whole notes. For example, in bar 5, play four quarter note Gs instead of playing a whole note. This will move that beat along and give your left hand a workout too.

# Here, There and Everywhere (page 58)

During The Beatles' much-ballyhooed run to the top of the pop pyramid, John Lennon and Paul McCartney never truly agreed about much. But one thing they happened to see eye-to-eye on is this lovely song, "Here, There and Everywhere." In his own biography, McCartney admitted it was one of his favorite Beatles tunes and, interestingly enough, in a *Playboy* interview, so did John Lennon. If it means anything, we feel the song is one of The Beatles best too! The top-notch UK rock magazine, *MOJO*, ranked this *Revolver* track as the fourth-greatest song of all time. So it's something of a unanimous decision: This song rocks. And while you're learning to play it on piano, you might be inclined to agree!

Even though the arrangement is pretty easy to play, watch out for those big chords in the left hand at the beginning and end. That squiggly line going up the side of the chord tells you to break apart the chord. Start with the bottom note and play up to the top note quickly. To blend the sound of the notes, hold down the sustain pedal.

Lennon and McCartney wrote a beautiful chord progression here. Want to try improvising? Okay, start by playing bars 4-5 with the left hand. Keep repeating that pattern: G, Am7, Bm, and C. Got that down? Now play the G Major scale (G-A-B-C-D-E-F#-G) in the right hand in eighth notes. Sounds neat, huh?

# How Deep Is the Ocean (page 62)

Love songs don't get any more resplendent, or more luminous, than Irving Berlin's 1932 classic. Yet while the melody was new in 1932, Berlin cribbed some of his older works for lyric ideas. Berlin composed "To My Mammy" for the Al Jolson motion picture *Mammy* two years earlier, and while he wasn't crazy about his own work, he took a few of the lines from it. He did the same with another tune from the 1930s, "How Much I Love You."

I've heard the tempo of this classic Irving Berlin song played really slow and breakneck fast. Try your hand at different tempos. You can also add a bit of swing and create more "bounce" in the melody.

Don't let your left hand go on vacation! There are two spots, one in the introduction and another on the last page, where the left hand crosses over the right hand. For example, in the second bar, play the E♭-G-C chord stemmed-up with your left hand.

# I Left My Heart in San Francisco (page 65)

Claramae Turner had the first crack at this enduring classic. Now, you might be asking yourself, "Who?" Admittedly, Turner isn't the biggest name in pop, mostly because she was an opera singer. But she did sing this song in 1960, when the song's writer, George Corey, presented it to her. On a side note, Corey, and his lyricist, spent a lot of time writing children's songs.

But it was, of course, Tony Bennett that first recorded the song, and made it his signature shortly after that, in 1962. Bennett came across the song via his accompanist Ralph Sharon, a former jazzman and a piano bandleader. He was constantly presented sheet music by aspiring writers, and one day, while looking for a shirt to bring on a tour, he came across the music to this song. He said, in an interview, "I thought, we're going to San Francisco, maybe I should bring this along." He did, and the rest is pop music history.

Take a look at the time signature changes on the second page. You're moving from 3/4 to 2/4, and then to 4/4 time for the rest of the song. Some really fun jazz chords are on the last page of this arrangement. Take them slow and arpeggiate the notes if the chords are too big for your hands.

Look ahead to the syncopation on the last page under the words "cis-co." The eighth note–quarter note-eighth note rhythm in the right hand creates a neat syncopation against the left-hand quarter notes. Practice this pattern a few times to really nail it when you get to that part.

Don't be fooled by the easy start to this song. Don't fall in the trap of starting off too fast, only to find yourself playing catch-up with your hands later, so take it slow in the beginning.

# I Will (page 70)

A rather simple love song, Paul McCartney's "I Will" took two days to record, and, surprisingly, 67 tries to get right, before finding its place on the band's epic *White* album. George wasn't around for this particular session, so he's not heard at all on this one. Legend has it that during these 67 takes the band took a number of giddy detours, especially in the wee hours of the morning, when they were feeling punchy. One of those outtakes, an improvised song based around the line "Can you take me back where I came from," a 28-second ditty, ended up between "Cry Baby Cry" and "Revolution #9."

Paul toyed with lyric ideas while studying in India; he even had a little help from Donovan on it. They spent a day meditating, and when they were done they started hashing out lyric ideas for the tune, which up to this time had eluded him. In the end, he scrapped the input and used a set of his own words to complete it. Incidentally, Paul admits he wrote the song for his future wife Linda Eastman.

There is fun interplay between the hands in this song. Don't be too heavy-handed when playing this gentle piece. The innocent simplicity of the song reminds me of two people on a park bench having a conversation. Keep that left hand steady while the syncopation of the right hand "floats" over the top. The D♭7 chord comes out of nowhere on the last page. Take a quick peek so you're not surprised.

It's easy to apply too much sustain pedal to this song. Can you play it without using the sustain pedal at all? This is a great way to learn legato playing. *Legato* means the notes sound connected (no break in sound).

# I'll Be There (page 73)

Of the many songs he sang so well, this one might be Michael Jackson's best vocal performance. Accompanied by big brother Jermaine, MJ was only 12 at the time of this recording, but his vocals show an amazing elegance and grace, accepting of course, his vocal flub when he tells his love to look over her "shoulders," and not "shoulder."

Written by Hal Davis, Willie Hutch, Bob West, and Motown prez Berry Gordy, the song is the Jackson 5's biggest selling single, as well as the best-selling single of Detroit-era Motown. (They later moved to Los Angeles.) It was the fourth #1 in a row for the boys, following "I Want You Back," "ABC," and "The Love You Save."

This Motown classic needs a strong steady beat to bring out the groove. Be careful not to drag when playing those steady eighth notes. Imagine a drummer playing with you, helping you to keep that steady eighth note pulse and enjoy the forward motion of the piece.

Do yourself a favor and take a look at the form before starting to play. Looking at the form is always a great way to get started with a song so that you don't miss something important while playing!

# I'll Have to Say I Love You in a Song (page 78)

Sometimes love songs are a great tool for kissing and making up. Just ask Jim Croce. He wrote this song for his wife Ingrid right after having an argument with her. Croce had just returned home from a tour and was apparently having trouble adjusting to home life. He and Ingrid started arguing, but instead of having a big blow up, Croce clamped up, retired to his basement, where he did his best writing, and came up with this one. The next morning, after he finished the tune, he sang it to his sleepy-eyed wife, who, though I can't confirm the fact, put her arms around him and forgave him for virtually everything. Sometimes great songwriters have *all* the luck.

This song moves along at a good clip. It helps to feel the beat in 2 rather than 4. Yes, it is written in 4/4 time, but feeling the beat in 2 is easier. Feel the accents on beats 1 and 3 while tapping your foot 1, 2, 3, 4.

Those straight lines over the notes in the bass clef are called *tenuto* marks. A *tenuto* marking can mean to hold the note for its full value or play the note slightly louder. In this case, the bass line needs to be strong so don't be shy!

# If (page 86)

Bread's principal songwriter David Gates loved to play music. He just didn't like the nightclub scene. The Tulsa native saved up his money and tried to make it on the road, but he got frustrated, tired, and fed up with the idea of doing all the work and having nothing to show for it. A few years into his career he discovered a songwriting crew around his new home in the "Valley" of California. The crew featured talent like Jerry Cole, Glen Campbell, and Leon Russell. Through these aspiring pros, Gates discovered session work existed and began to understand the demand for quality songwriting. He loved the idea of writing music for a living, without the hassle of touring to bring him down. The prospect excited him and he began to write with renewed enthusiasm. Demo work opened up, and so people began to ask him for songs. At this point, even before he teamed up with his future songwriting partner James Griffin, he knew he was more comfortable behind the scenes. And it would only be a matter of time before the hits started coming.

You can really express yourself with this song. Have fun with dynamics too! In each bar of the introduction, start playing the left hand softly, get a little louder (*crescendo*), then play softly again (*decrescendo*).

The last four bars of the song require a two-handed effort. The straight lines between the left and right hands are telling you to use your right hand to play the chord, then jump down and play those left hand notes, before coming up to play the next chord with your right hand.

# *If I Loved You* (page 90)

Don't you just love a great show tune? This one is from the 1945 Rodgers and Hammerstein production *Carousel*, starring Shirley Jones and Gordon MacRae. The song, in which MacRae and Jones tentatively profess their young love for each other, is like a delicate flower, beautiful in its naïveté and lyricism. The song actually stemmed from a few lines derived from *Lilion*, the French play that inspired *Carousel*. The French version of the story was popular in its own right much earlier in the 20th century, but for English-speaking audiences, the Rodgers and Hammerstein version takes the cake. The song was first recorded by John Raitt and Jan Clayton back in 1945, when it was originally released as a single. Since then, many have taken a crack at capturing the same delicate naïveté. That many have succeeded attests to the fact that the song itself simply works. Hear for yourself!

No, you're not seeing things; those are two G clefs at the beginning of the song. The introduction starts with both hands above middle C. Don't miss the bass clef when it comes in at the top of the second page. In several places the left hand moves between treble clef and bass clef. The first of these is at the bottom of the second page, so watch out!

The time changes from 2/4 to 4/4. Remember, 4/4 time is like two bars of 2/4 time. Also be aware of the key change from D to C Major. Don't get derailed by the shift in tempo. Even though the allegretto introduction is played moderately fast, the refrain slows down quite a bit.

# *Isn't It Romantic?* (page 81)

We could spend hours paging through the Great American Songbook, filled with all those super romantic classics. One song that you'll be hard-pressed not to find in anything that calls itself a "Great American Songbook" is this legendary work, the Rodgers and Hart gem, "Isn't It Romantic?" Some critics have even called this one "the perfect song," and who are we to argue? First introduced in the 1932 film *Love Me Tonight*, sung by Jeanette MacDonald and Maurice Chevalier, this tune has it all. Many of the very best singers in American music history tried their hand at singing this one, including Ella Fitzgerald, Roberta Flack, and Tony Bennett.

The cut-time time signature ( ¢ ) gives this song a half note pulse. Use the half notes in the arrangement to keep a calm, slow tempo. At the refrain, "Isn't it romantic," you can pick up the pace.

Want to jazz up this song? Try applying a swing, a long-short pattern, to the eighth notes. You can also try playing the quarter notes a bit shorter. Don't play them staccato, just a bit more "bouncy" to get a "plucking" bass-note feel.

# Lady *(page 114)*

Lionel Richie (yes, Nicole's father) came from a hardcore soul background in Tuskegee, Alabama. The Commodores (where he first came to the public's attention) were one of Motown's most successful bands in the 1970s and '80s. They even opened for the Jackson 5 in 1972, when they originally signed with the label. But Richie always seemed to have bigger plans, and he began writing songs for other artists. This one became his first huge hit for another performer. Perhaps you know him? It was Kenny Rogers. Rogers originally released "Lady" in 1980, and it zoomed up four separate charts, peaking at #1 on Billboard's Hot 100, Adult Contemporary, and the Top Country singles charts, and even hit the Top 40 on the Black singles chart. That would be called a quadruple "crossover," not to be confused with the heart bypass operation with a similar name.

Often composers are looking for new ways to play with the accents in a song. Richie achieves this by switching between 2/4 and 4/4 time. This basically creates a bar of 6/4 and it adds a lot more space to the melody.

The *8va* at the end of the song tells you to play the notes under that bracket an octave higher. ***Note:*** If the bracket were below the notes, you would play them an octave lower.

# Longer *(page 118)*

Dan Fogelberg had a great outlook on life (he died in 2007). He wrote some terrific songs, which altogether sold over 15 million records. And he always maintained a great sense of humor. Case in point, he referred to "Longer," as the track that put him on elevators. "I wrote it on a vacation in Maui in 1979," he wrote in the liner notes to *Portrait,* his boxed set, "while lounging on a hammock one night looking up at the stars." Now isn't that how you'd imagine a lovely, laid-back song like this one would get written? "It just seemed this song was drifting around the universe, saw me, and decided I would give it a good home." You sure did, Dan. You sure did.

Be sure to note the two bass clefs at the beginning of the piano accompaniment, and read the notes accordingly. The down-stemmed half notes in the left hand at bar 5 tell you to hold those notes down while playing the rest of the notes that fall in those two beats.

There is some challenging syncopation on the second page at "showers in the springs" that you should practice a few times. Use the steady eighth notes in the left-hand part to keep the rhythm accurate.

You can express yourself by creating your own solo by going back to the introduction between verses. The intro that is written has some really nice motion in both left and right hands. Use this as a springboard for your own solo. For instance, try playing the left-hand pattern at bar 5 under bars 1-4.

# Love Me Tender *(page 122)*

Talk about a footnote — in cinema, that is! *Love Me Tender,* the movie in which this song was introduced, was Elvis Presley's acting debut. In the 1956 film, Presley plays Clint Reno, the brother of a Confederate soldier. After learning that Reno's brother died in battle, Presley married his girlfriend. When his brother actually proved to be alive, and found his way back home after the war, you can imagine the surprise. Let's just say Elvis isn't as good a sharpshooter as he was a rock and roller, and let's also say that this film isn't quite as timeless as the song it so flatteringly featured.

This song was adapted by Elvis from an old Civil War ballad "Aura Lee." Enjoy the introduction by playing it much slower than you might otherwise. Let the chords ring out. You can even try *arpeggiating* (breaking up) the notes of the chords.

The space and simplicity of the chords make this song a perfect candidate for some improvisation. Try humming the melody to yourself while playing the left-hand part. Embellish the notes of the melody (with your voice) by changing the rhythm or going up or down a step from a note. For instance, instead of "Love me ten-der," try "Love me ten-ten-der." See how we repeated the note twice? You wouldn't do this while singing, but it works great over an instrumental section.

# Loving You (page 124)

Do you know what the *whistle register* is? It's the range of the human voice above the modal register and falsetto register. Something weird happens to the vocal cords, though no one is really sure what that is because they are difficult to film when they're actually producing a pitch this high. If you want to know what the whistle register sounds like, check out Minnie Riperton's version of the song.

Riperton had an eye-popping five and a half octave vocal range, which is pretty extraordinary, especially for a pop/rock/soul/funk singer. A little digging into Minnie's background, though, does reveal some operatic training, which makes sense; you simply can't produce these incredible sounds without a little preparation! That would be like trying to run a marathon without doing any training to prepare. It hurts just thinking about it.

Take it slow! This should be played with a laid-back feel. You also want to add a bit of swing to the eighth notes. You can almost think of this as a slow stride. Get your left hand ready for those triplets on the second page. Do you see the dotted quarter note tied to the eighth note in the next bar? This is creating a syncopation between the left and right hands. You can also think of the rhythm as two eighth notes on beat 4. So, the F on beat 3 is the first eighth note and the A-C is the second. The same type of syncopation happens in bar 3.

The eighth notes in the second-to-last bar should be played as "straight" or "even" eighth notes. So, don't swing those notes!

# Misty (page 111)

You don't often hear of a song earning two inductions to the GRAMMY Hall of Fame. "Misty" is one incredible exception. Back in 1954 Erroll Garner recorded an instrumental version, with lyrics tacked on by Johnny Burke. That rendition was inducted in 1991. Co-opted by creamy-voiced pop singer Johnny Mathis in 1959, the song earned a second GRAMMY induction, this time in 2002 as a Traditional Pop Song. In the world of jazz standards, "Misty" has attained legendary status, thanks to mega-popular renditions by Billy Eckstine, Ella Fitzgerald, and Sarah Vaughan, not to mention Ol' Blue Eyes and Julie London. As a pianist, you don't have to choose which version you prefer. We're pretty sure you'll love every note you play.

Take a moment to play some of those rich, beautiful chords spread throughout this piece. There is a gorgeous walk-up on the second page under "You can say that you're leading..." Picking apart these big chords will help you learn the arrangement faster and improve your chord knowledge, which is always a good thing!

This piece has a nice mix of duple and triple rhythms. Eighth notes are duple, and triplets and quarter-note triplets are triple. Moving back and forth between duple and triple rhythms can pose a challenge. To prepare yourself, tap a steady quarter-note beat with one hand. In your other hand, move between tapping eighth notes, triplets, and quarter note triplets.

# More Than Words (page 126)

Extreme's founding members, Gary Cherone and Nuno Bettencourt started out their professional rock lives as big-time noisemakers. In their hometown of Boston back in 1986 and 1987, they were two-time winners of the top "Metal/Hard Rock Act" prize at the Boston Music Awards. Bettencourt and Cherone routinely wrote blistering, metal-tinged rock characterized by Bettencourt's sizzling shred guitar and Cherone's imposing vocals. Their debut did well enough to warrant a follow-up album and in 1990 they reased *Extreme II: Pornograffiti*.

That album featured the acoustic ballad "More Than Words." The tender, exquisitely performed love song, a slow dance/prom night staple, soared to #1 in the spring on 1991 and made Extreme a household name.

However, both Bettencourt and Cherone have blamed Extreme's downturn on the song. The cold hard truth is that this song may have pulled in greater numbers of pop music fans, but its success also gave Extreme the reputation of being a light rock act, with feathery vocals and pretty acoustic guitars. The misconception sent their serious fans elsewhere and sent the band down the path of playing the kind of music they didn't enjoy.

Get in the groove by heating up the beat. Count the 4/4 time signature with a feeling of eight for more precision. Count it this way, however: *one and two and three and four and.* The *one and* method labels the *offbeats,* an important part of any groove!

At the core, this smooth serenade relies on its groove and vibe and really is "more than words." The easy yet passionate blend of music and words create the "more."

# My Funny Valentine (page 132)

*Babes in Arms,* a 1937 musical by Richard Rodgers and Lorenz Hart, concerns a teenager who puts on a show with his friends in order to avoid being sent to a work farm. Yet, from rather ordinary origins come extraordinary results, and today it's considered a classic. One only has to look at the enduring songs it spawned to see just how amazing the work really is. In addition to "My Funny Valentine," the musical featured "Where or When," "The Lady Is a Tramp," and "I Wish I Were in Love Again," among others. When the jazz world caught wind of "My Funny Valentine," they took it on a long, strange trip. This is especially true in the hands of matinee idol trumpeter turned drug addict Chet Baker. His emotionally remote, spectacularly distant rendition of the love song was like hearing the echo of a song, rather than the song itself, but in total, intimate clarity. Baker lived a hard life, though, in contrast to the smooth sexiness of his most famous cover, and died after falling out of the window of an Amsterdam hotel.

Watch your clefs! There are two treble clefs in the introduction. The hands get close together, but that's all right because there are no collisions here. Watch for the bass clef before the lyric begins.

For almost 16 bars, the right hand plays by itself. If you want to fill in some notes with your left hand, use chord roots. The first chord is C minor, so the root is C. For B♭7, the root is B♭.

On the last page, you come across the words *molto espress.,* short for *molto espressivo,* which in Italian means "very expressive." Tap into your romantic side and give this section a lot of expression.

# My Heart Will Go On (page 142)

Lyricist Will Jennings' name comes up a lot for a guy few of us consider to be a star. He began his career in the '70s, with one of his first hits, "Looks Like We Made It." A few years later he had a hand in writing "Up Where We Belong," the Oscar-winning song from the motion picture *An Officer and a Gentleman*. And a few years after that, he finished Eric Clapton's lyrics for "Tears in Heaven," when EC had trouble finishing the heartbreaking song about the death of his young son. Throughout the last four decades, Jennings' name pops up in some very prominent places, as a man responsible for some of our generation's most popular and successful works. He collaborated with *Titanic* film scorer James Horner on "My Heart Will Go On," after hitting it fairly big with Horner on a previous film, *An American Tail: Fievel Goes West.* Other Jennings' partners include Steve Winwood, B.B. King, and Roy Orbison.

Take a peek at those big *arpeggios* (broken chords) in the left hand on the second page under the lyrics "Near, far, wherever you are." Take them slowly and use your sustain pedal. Bring that pinky along with the other fingers. In other words, don't keep your hand wide open throughout the entire bar because this creates a lot of tension in your hand.

Be mindful of the key change to F minor on the second-to-last page. There's some nice writing here! So often the modulation in popular songs is by half or whole step. This modulation moves up a major 3rd, which creates enormous "lift" to the song. I bet you already heard that though!

# Put Your Head on My Shoulder (page 148)

In the late '50s, Paul Anka took full advantage of rock 'n' roll. He smoothed out the sounds of raucous vibes and took his creamy sounding voice to the top of the charts. But Anka's phenomenal success was very nearly cut short. In 1959 Anka appeared in rock promoter Irvin Feld's biggest show of all. It featured Buddy Holly, The Big Bopper, Ritchie Valens, Dion and the Belmonts, and others. Fate spared Anka from perishing in a plane crash along with Holly, The Big Bopper, and Valens, in what has famously come to be known as "The Day the Music Died."

Above the lyric in bar 4 you'll notice *N.C.,* which stands for "No Chord." This tells you to play only the melody, without a chord. If you want to fill out the sound, double the melody with your left hand an octave lower.

The eighth notes are written as *swing eighths,* which means they would have a "long-short" rhythm. However, did you know that you can change the amount of swing that you apply? In fact, as you listen to more pianists, especially jazz pianists, you can start to tell them apart by how they swing their eighth notes. So, channel your inner jazz pianist and play around with those swing eighths!

# Some Enchanted Evening (page 137)

By extremely unofficial count, "Some Enchanted Evening," a song featured in Rodgers and Hammerstein's musical *South Pacific,* has been covered by, well, everyone. Versions were hammered out by artists as widely known and varied as Frank Sinatra, Willie Nelson, Bon Jovi, Al Jolson, The Temptations, and Harrison Ford, who sang it in the motion picture *American Graffiti!* In one particularly memorable version, Bert, Ernie's buddy on *Sesame Street,* sang the song to '70s TV star Connie Stevens. Such is the fate of a brilliant piece of music, which debuted in a timeless show, and became a classic faster than you could say "Nellie Forbush." (For the uninitiated, Nellie was the love interest in the show.)

Dust off your sustain pedal, 'cause you're going to need it for this wonderful arrangement. Take a look half way down the third page, under the lyric "dreams." The C chord in the left hand and whole note C in the right hand are sustained while playing the rest of the bar. Start by playing the chord, press the sustain pedal, and then play the Gs.

Don't turn those quarter note triplets into a different rhythm! At the top of the second page, the notes under "...somehow you...(know)" there is a quarter note triplet figure. This rhythm is repeated many times throughout the piece, usually coupled with two notes in the left hand. The rhythm that is created is what is called *three-against-two*. This means the three quarter notes in the right hand are played in the span of two quarter note beats in the left hand. To practice this rhythm, tap three beats in your right hand while counting, "1 and 2 and 3 and" adding in your left hand, tapping on beat 1 and the "and" of beat 2.

# Sunrise, Sunset *(page 152)*

The musical *Fiddler on the Roof* debuted in 1964, and would become the first Broadway musical to surpass 3,000 performances. It won a passel of Tony® Awards and held the record for longest running Broadway play until a little production named *Grease* elbowed it out of the top spot. Composer Jerry Bock and lyricist Sheldon Harnick, the songwriting duo behind Pulitzer Prize winners *Fiorello!* and *She Loves Me* teamed up with librettist Joseph Stein to create a musical based on Sholom Aleichem's stories. Zero Mostel gets top billing for his role as the aged dairyman (and father of five girls) Tevye, who struggles to honor tradition amid the changing climate of his Russian village. "Sunrise, Sunset" is one of a handful of delightful numbers in this musical.

The D7 chord on the second page under "they" provides a nice transition back into the melody. However, the left-hand crossover might get tricky. Hold down the sustain pedal through both bars to get the full effect.

Keep this spirited piece light, taking care not to play too heavily. Enjoy the whimsical nature of the melody and accompaniment while propelling this waltz with a strong, steady rhythm.

# Three Times a Lady *(page 156)*

In 1977, the year of the Sex Pistols' epic punk anthem "God Save the Queen," Lionel Richie and The Commodores' breezy ballad "Easy" lost the Best R&B Song GRAMMY to Leo Sayer's "You Make Me Feel Like Dancing," which tells you something about the GRAMMYs that year not really having their finger on the pulse of things. Rumor has it that Richie was embarrassed by the slight, and he set out to write uber-commercial ballads in an attempt to never lose an R&B prize again. By all appearances, he succeeded. Following the template set by "Easy," Richie and The Commodores soared with a heaping handful of hits: "Still" and "Sail On," and later Richie hit big with solo hits like "Truly," "Hello," "Stuck on You," and "Penny Lover."

Breathe like a singer and don't rush the melody. Right after the lyrics "must say out loud" there is a nice pause in the music before coming back in with, "You're once, twice..." There is another pause like this later, before "When we are together..." Don't chop off the rests because they add a lot of space and feeling to the piece. Instead, take a breath during that pause and come back into the melody relaxed.

On the last page, before the last lyric, you'll see the tempo indication *rall.* This stands for *rallentando* and tells you to gradually get slower. You can get slower all the way to the last note. Really express yourself here.

## Truly *(page 162)*

Lionel Richie recorded his first solo album for Motown over the course of nine months, yielding a clutch of big hits, including "Truly." He often spoke about the old, brown, beat-up piano he used in the studio, and how it must have been good luck. He might be right. It was the same piano Carole King played on her legendary album *Tapestry.*

This song is dripping with emotion. Keep it slow and be free with the tempo. Pushing and pulling the tempo on a song like this helps to give it a "breathing" quality. Try starting off slow, but get just a bit faster within a bar, then slow back down before the next bar. Think of the song as alive and breathing with every note you play.

The *fermata* ⌒ lets you hold the note for as long as you wish. The introduction has a fermata over the G/C chords. Experiment by holding those chords for longer than you might otherwise. The pause helps to create tension and interest.

The second-to-last bar includes notes beamed between the treble and bass clef. You can play these notes with only the left hand, or bring your right hand into the game for some of them if you wish.

## The Way You Look Tonight *(page 166)*

Dorothy Fields, who wrote the lyrics to this lovely Jerome Kern tune, was one of the first women to work successfully as a lyricist on Tin Pan Alley. Fields graduated in 1923 from the Benjamin Franklin School for Girls in New York City, where she excelled in English, drama, and basketball, and had her poems published in the school's literary magazine. A few years later she began writing songs, and got a job as a lyricist at Mills Music, where one of her first assignments was to write the lyrics for a tune commemorating aviator Ruth Elder's attempt to cross the Atlantic Ocean. She moved to Hollywood where she met Kern, and they began collaborating, first on the film soundtrack to *Roberta,* and then on 1936's *Swing Time,* where "The Way You Look Tonight" first appeared. The tune, crooned by Fred Astaire, won an Academy Award for Best Song. As an interesting footnote, Fields and Kern were hired in the '40s to write the words and music to a musical dedicated to sharpshooter Annie Oakley, though Kern died before the two embarked on the project. They were instead replaced by Irving Berlin, who wrote both the words and the music, quite successfully!

This arrangement lets you really have some fun with the tempo. The *rall.* in the introduction stands for *rallentando* and tells you to gradually play slower. You see this again at "glow just thinking of you." At the *a tempo* go back to the original tempo. Have fun experimenting with speeding up and slowing down where you choose!

Articulation, long and short attacks on a note, can really add some flair to your playing. Try applying a short staccato articulation to the inner chords in the beginning under "Some day when I'm awfully low."

## What the World Needs Now Is Love *(page 169)*

Composer Burt Bacharach and lyricist Hal David wrote many songs that were recorded by Dionne Warwick, including "Do You Know the Way to San Jose," "Walk on By," and "Anyone Who Had a Heart." Strangely enough, this song was not one of them. Not that the songwriting partnership didn't try. Recalls Bacharach in an interview with *Record Collector* magazine: "Dionne rejected that song. She might have thought it was too preachy and I thought Dionne was probably right."

Lyricist David remembers what happened too: "We showed the song to Dionne Warwick, who had recorded many of our songs, and it is the only song of ours that she ever turned down." Bacharach and David then turned to Liberty recording artist Jackie DeShannon: "Once I heard Jackie sing four bars of it," said Bacharach, "I thought, this is great! She had such a great voice." But the partnership with DeShannon didn't last; this would be the only hit they had with her. On a side note, The Beatles took advantage of the feel-good hippie vibe of the era, when they wrote their own tune along the same lines. You might remember it? "All You Need Is Love."

This song is another lovely waltz. The trick is to play the chords with a gentle touch and a bit of a jazz feel. You'll really notice this on the last eighth note in bar 1 before moving to the next bar. To get that jazz feel, think of the eighth note as being a little shorter. In other words, it should leap into the next bar with more bounce. Or, think of the rhythm as a long-short pattern.

Don't be afraid to express yourself with this song. Shake loose by playing around with the rhythm of the melody. Heck, you can even try taking your own instrumental solo!

# Woman (page 172)

In "Girl," a track on the Beatles' *Rubber Soul* in 1965, John Lennon proved you could be in the wholesome Fab Four and still burn with sexual desire. There was a tremendous intimacy in everything Lennon did, and that tension made him a great singer. Teenagers of both sexes were burning with that same desire, the kind of desire the kids might have felt, but their parents totally missed. Anyway, Lennon referred to his 1980 track "Woman" as a sequel of sorts to "Girl," kind of a grown-up look at the same burning intimacy. The track appeared on Lennon's ultra-committed, kiss-on-the-cover *Double Fantasy* album. Ironically, this album came out just three weeks before Lennon's murder in December of 1980. Just after his death, his label Geffen re-released "Imagine" as a single. With grief worldwide reaching a crescendo, the album went to #1, and "Woman," the second single off the record, also did well as a follow-up to the #1 single, "(Just Like) Starting Over."

Even though this song is played slowly, don't let it lose its drive. Because you have a lot of half note chords in the left hand, it's up to the right hand to move things right along.

You have choices at the end. You can play the optional ending or fade out. Fading out is an art all by itself on the piano. Each time you repeat the section, get a little softer but try not to lose the tone of the notes.

# You Must Love Me (page 175)

After Andrew Lloyd Webber and Tim Rice's *Evita* knocked 'em dead at the Broadway box offices in the late '70s, a film version was made in 1997. You know, the one Madonna was in. This song was written specifically for the film version and in 1997, it ended up winning an Oscar® for Best Original Song in a Film. Rice and Webber had written together successfully and often, but had not collaborated in 13 years before coming together for this one tune.

Watch out for colliding fingers on the bottom of the first page at "Certainties disappear." Play the half notes with the right hand and hold down the pedal to make it easier to move between these notes. Play the F-D and F-B♭ with your right hand while keeping the flow.

Triplets and eighth notes might slow you down. Take a look at the three-against-two rhythm at "Deep in my heart." See the notes on "Some Enchanted Evening" for some tips on playing this rhythm.

You can make a grand statement with the ritard at the bottom of the second page. Have fun slowing down the tempo there before returning to the original speed. You can also play with the tempo during the instrumental section to add your own personal touch to the song.

# *You're in My Heart* (page 184)

Ah, Rod the Sod! Depending on who you ask, this song is either about his favorite soccer team ("You're Celtic United, but baby I've decided you're the best team I've ever seen") or it's about his wife at the time, Swedish model Britt Ekland. Both are likely true. It's been noted that during his tour he'd kick soccer balls out into the crowd. Of course, he's also been known as an audacious womanizer who often wrote about his conquests in song, and there were many! It could also mean that his wife was more gratifying than the soccer team he so loved, which, if you're Rod Stewart, could be quite a lot.

With the swing eighths, this song has almost a little bit of a jazz feel to it. It helps to feel the backbeat of this song to get the full effect. If you listen to the original, you'll hear the guitarist accenting beats 2 and 4. This is the backbeat. Try humming the melody of the song while you tap on beats 2 and 4. Now apply that feeling as you play your right hand.

Don't miss the key change at the second ending.  Also take a look at the first and second endings on the last page to catch those key changes as well! You're moving around a lot in this song, so watch out!

# *Your Song* (page 178)

Back in 1970, Three Dog Night was one of the rock scene's hottest acts. In fact, they were so big, young Elton John, unknown in the States at the time, had been their opening act. Elton was writing fairly prolifically, and Three Dog Night had taken to his material. They covered his song "Lady Samantha," and did a version of "Your Song" before Elton himself released it officially. But when things started to break for Elton, Three Dog Night chose not to release the song on their 1970 album *It Ain't Easy.* Instead they let Elton release "Your Song" as a single, in an effort to get their opening act off the ground. The plan worked both ways. Elton skyrocketed, and Three Dog Night had no trouble getting airplay with songs like "Joy to the World," "One," and "Just an Old Fashioned Love Song."

Playing this song is a rock pianist's dream. Sir Elton sure knows how to rock out and this song is a testament to that! Pay attention to the time signature changes on almost every page of this arrangement. To get the feel, start with the melody and the left hand. It helps to see where the lyrics and left hand "link up" because in rock piano, the left hand drives the beat.

To effectively learn a challenging arrangement such as this, it helps to break it into sections and practice those sections over and over again. You probably already knew that, but here's some advice: Start with a different section each day. If you always start at the beginning, that's the part of the song that will sound the strongest. You'll be able to play the entire song confidently by shifting the sections that you practice!

# Misty

Words by Johnny Burke
Music by Erroll Garner

# Lady

Words and Music by Lionel Richie

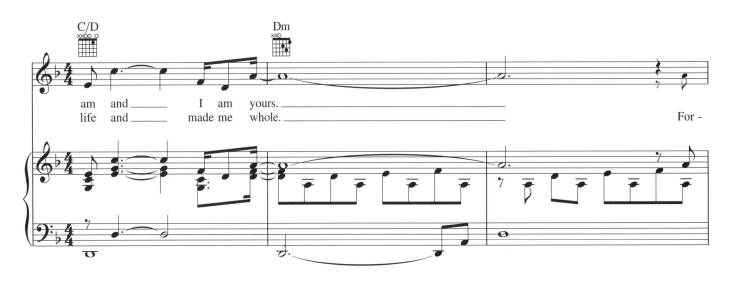

# Longer

Words and Music by Dan Fogelberg

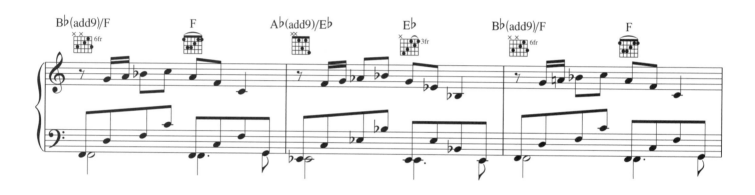

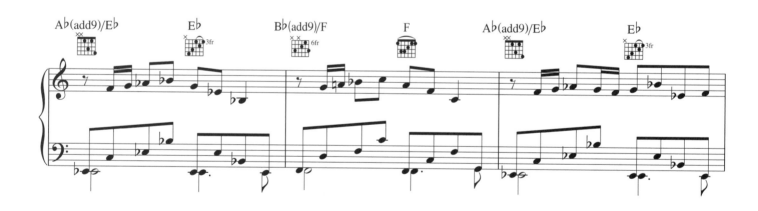

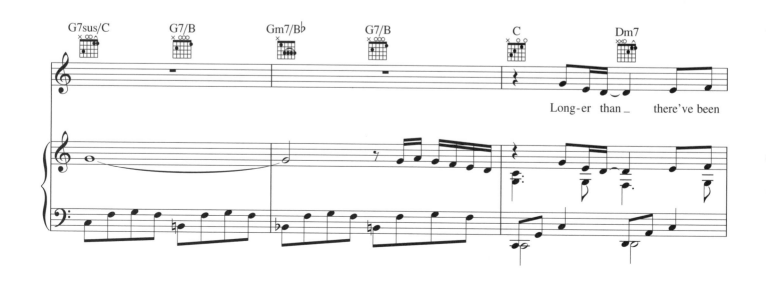

# Love Me Tender

Words and Music by Elvis Presley and Vera Matson

**Moderately slow**

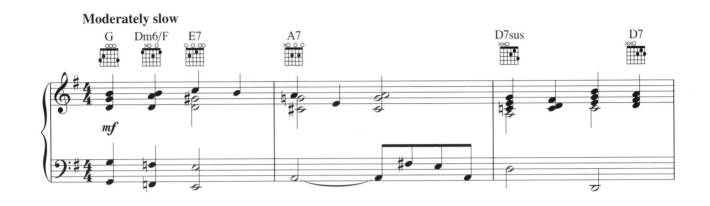

Love me ten - der, love me sweet,
Love me ten - der, love me long,
Love me ten - der, love me dear,
When at last my dreams come true,

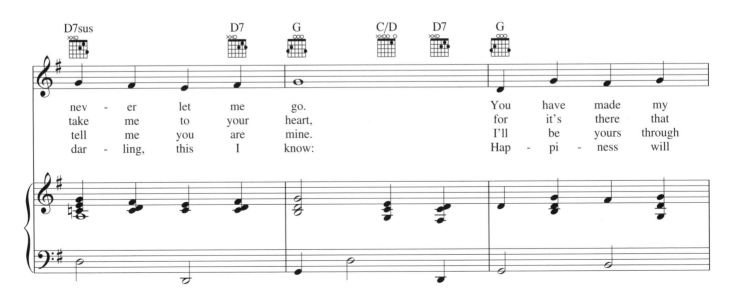

nev - er let me go. You have made my
take me to your heart, for it's there that
tell me you are mine. I'll be yours through
dar - ling, this I know: Hap - pi - ness will

# Loving You

Words and Music by Jerry Leiber and Mike Stoller

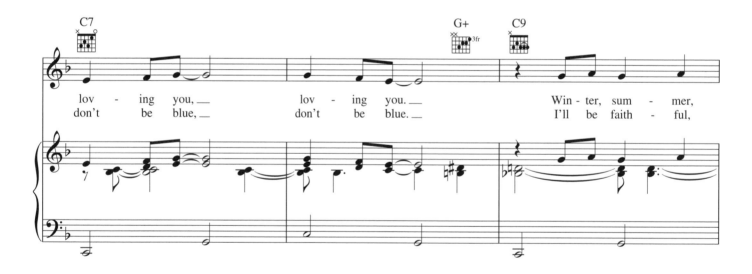

# More Than Words

Words and Music by Nuno Bettencourt and Gary Cherone

*Recorded a half step lower.*

# My Funny Valentine

from BABES IN ARMS
Words by Lorenz Hart
Music by Richard Rodgers

# Some Enchanted Evening

from SOUTH PACIFIC
Lyrics by Oscar Hammerstein II
Music by Richard Rodgers

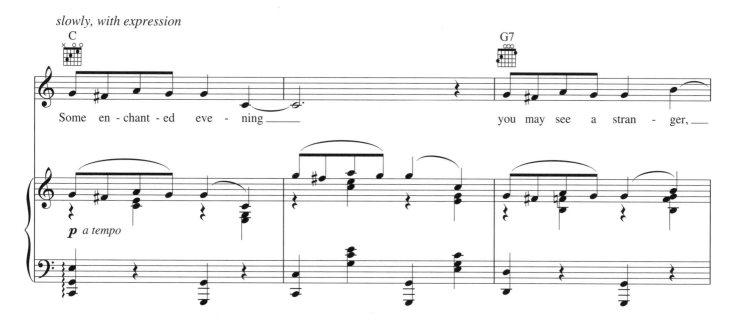

Some en-chant-ed eve-ning ____ you may see a stran-ger, ____

____ you may see a stran-ger ____ a-cross a

# My Heart Will Go On

(Love Theme from 'Titanic')
from the Paramount and Twentieth Century Fox Motion Picture TITANIC
Music by James Horner
Lyric by Will Jennings

# Put Your Head on My Shoulder

Words and Music by Paul Anka

Put your head on my shoul - der, hold me in your arms, ba - by. Squeeze me oh so tight, show me that you love me too. _____ Put your lips close to

# Sunrise, Sunset

from the Musical FIDDLER ON THE ROOF
Words by Sheldon Harnick
Music by Jerry Bock

**Moderately slow Waltz tempo**

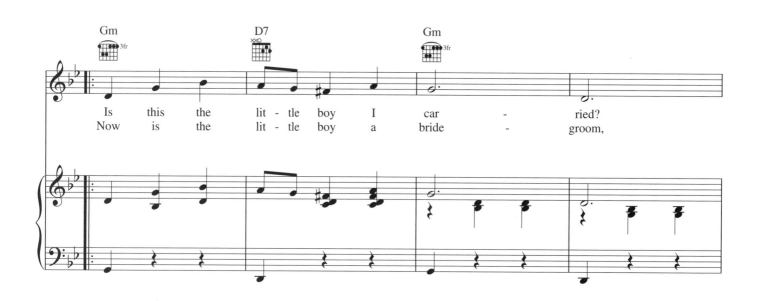

Is this the lit - tle boy I car - ried?
Now is the lit - tle boy a bride - groom,

Is this the lit - tle girl at play?
now is the lit - tle girl a bride?

I don't re -
Un - der the

# Three Times a Lady

Words and Music by Lionel Richie

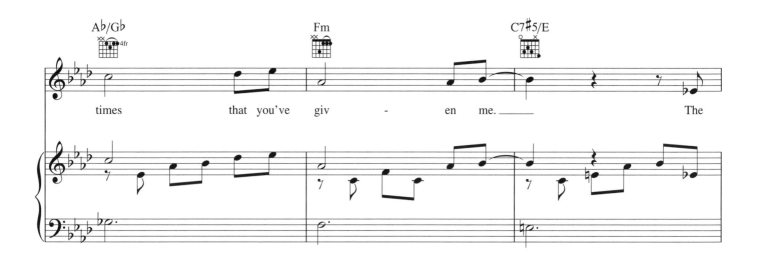

# *Truly*

Words and Music by Lionel Richie

# The Way You Look Tonight

Words by Dorothy Fields
Music by Jerome Kern

# What the World Needs Now Is Love

Lyric by Hal David
Music by Burt Bacharach

**With a Jazz Waltz feel**

# Woman

Words and Music by John Lennon

# You Must Love Me

from the Cinergi Motion Picture EVITA
Words by Tim Rice
Music by Andrew Lloyd Webber

**Flowing**

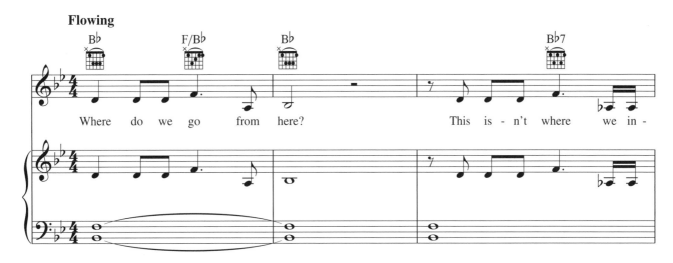

Where do we go from here? This is - n't where we in -

tend - ed to be. __ We had it all, __ you be - lieved __ in me, __ I be -

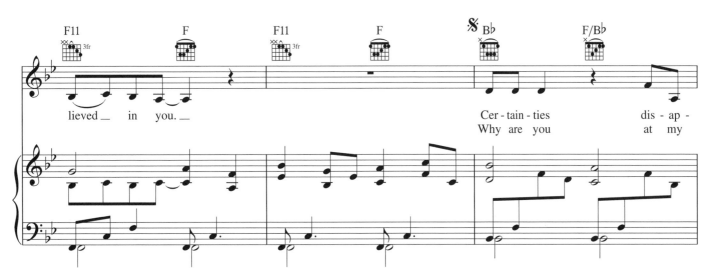

lieved __ in you. __
Cer - tain - ties                    dis - ap -
Why are you                    at my

# Your Song

Words and Music by Elton John and Bernie Taupin

# You're in My Heart

Words and Music by Rod Stewart

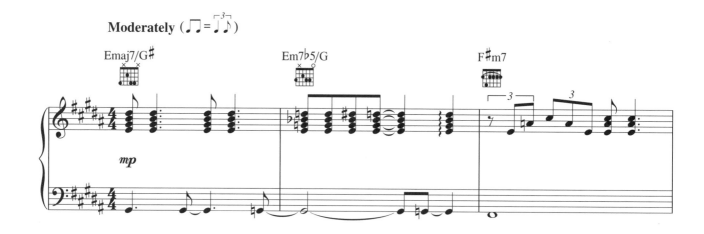

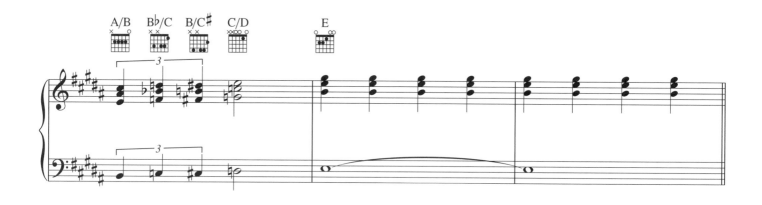

I did-n't know ___ what day it was ___ when you walked ___

I took all ___ those hab-its of yours that in the be -